This Playbook Belongs To Coach:

_____

Month Of:_____

SUN	MON	TUES	WED	THURS	FRI	SAT

Month Of:_____

SUN	MON	TUES	WED	THURS	FRI	SAT

Month Of:_____

SUN	MON	TUES	WED	THURS	FRI	SAT

Month Of:_____

SUN	MON	TUES	WED	THURS	FRI	SAT

Month Of:_____

SUN	MON	TUES	WED	THURS	FRI	SAT

Month Of:_____

SUN	MON	TUES	WED	THURS	FRI	SAT

Month Of:_____

SUN	MON	TUES	WED	THURS	FRI	SAT

Month Of:_____

SUN	MON	TUES	WED	THURS	FRI	SAT

Month Of:_____

SUN	MON	TUES	WED	THURS	FRI	SAT

Month Of:_____

SUN	MON	TUES	WED	THURS	FRI	SAT

Month Of:_____

SUN	MON	TUES	WED	THURS	FRI	SAT

Month Of:_____

SUN	MON	TUES	WED	THURS	FRI	SAT

Index of Games

1 _____
Opponent   Date   Location   W/L   Score

2 _____
Opponent   Date   Location   W/L   Score

3 _____
Opponent   Date   Location   W/L   Score

4 _____
Opponent   Date   Location   W/L   Score

5 _____
Opponent   Date   Location   W/L   Score

6 _____
Opponent   Date   Location   W/L   Score

7 _____
Opponent   Date   Location   W/L   Score

8 _____
Opponent   Date   Location   W/L   Score

Index of Games

9 _____ _____ _____ _____ _____
   Opponent   Date   Location   W/L   Score

10 _____ _____ _____ _____ _____
   Opponent   Date   Location   W/L   Score

11 _____ _____ _____ _____ _____
   Opponent   Date   Location   W/L   Score

12 _____ _____ _____ _____ _____
   Opponent   Date   Location   W/L   Score

13 _____ _____ _____ _____ _____
   Opponent   Date   Location   W/L   Score

14 _____ _____ _____ _____ _____
   Opponent   Date   Location   W/L   Score

15 _____ _____ _____ _____ _____
   Opponent   Date   Location   W/L   Score

16 _____ _____ _____ _____ _____
   Opponent   Date   Location   W/L   Score

Index of Games

17 _____   _____   _____   _____   _____
      Opponent   Date   Location   W/L   Score

18 _____   _____   _____   _____   _____
      Opponent   Date   Location   W/L   Score

19 _____   _____   _____   _____   _____
      Opponent   Date   Location   W/L   Score

20 _____   _____   _____   _____   _____
      Opponent   Date   Location   W/L   Score

21 _____   _____   _____   _____   _____
      Opponent   Date   Location   W/L   Score

22 _____   _____   _____   _____   _____
      Opponent   Date   Location   W/L   Score

23 _____   _____   _____   _____   _____
      Opponent   Date   Location   W/L   Score

24 _____   _____   _____   _____   _____
      Opponent   Date   Location   W/L   Score

Index of Games

25	Opponent	Date	Location	W/L	Score
26	Opponent	Date	Location	W/L	Score
27	Opponent	Date	Location	W/L	Score
28	Opponent	Date	Location	W/L	Score
29	Opponent	Date	Location	W/L	Score
30	Opponent	Date	Location	W/L	Score
31	Opponent	Date	Location	W/L	Score
32	Opponent	Date	Location	W/L	Score

Index of Games

	Opponent	Date	Location	W/L	Score
33					
34					
35					
36					
37					
38					
39					
40					

Player Roster

HOME #	AWAY #	LAST NAME	FIRST NAME	YEAR	EMERGENCY CONTACT

Player Roster

HOME #	AWAY #	LAST NAME	FIRST NAME	YEAR	EMERGENCY CONTACT

Play Name:_____

_____
_____
_____
_____
_____
_____
_____
_____

Play Name:_____

Play Name:_____

Play Name:_____

Play Name:_____

_____

_____

_____

_____

_____

_____

_____

_____

Play Name:_____

Play Name:_____

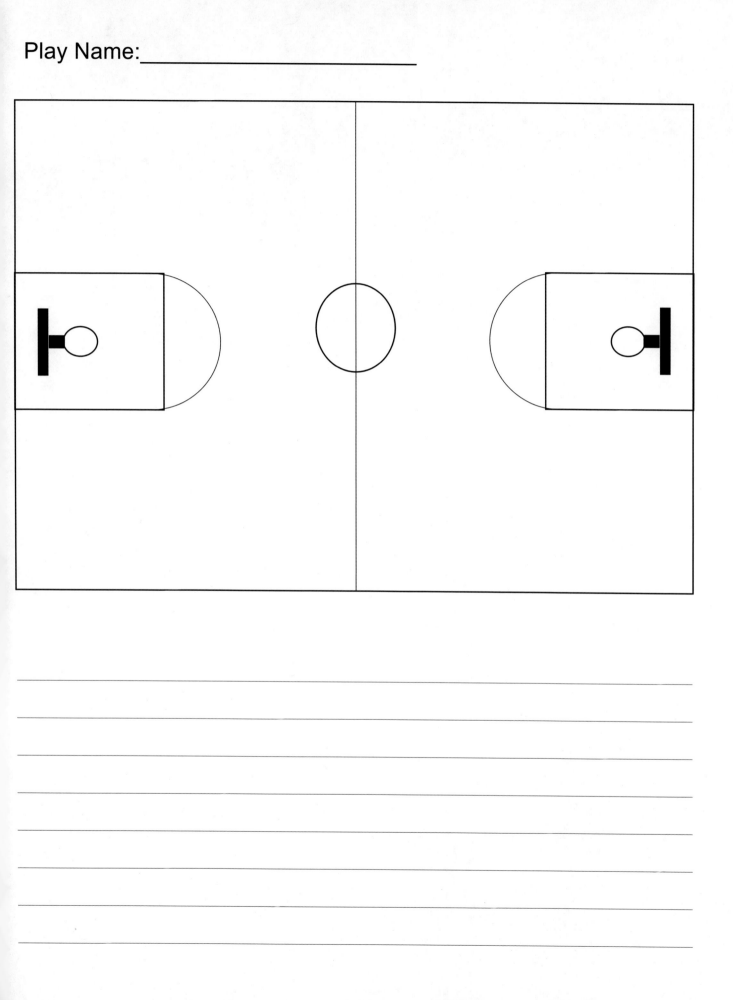

Play Name:_____

Play Name:_____

Play Name:_____

_____
_____
_____
_____
_____
_____
_____
_____

Play Name:_____

_____

_____

_____

_____

_____

_____

_____

_____

Play Name:_____

Play Name:_____

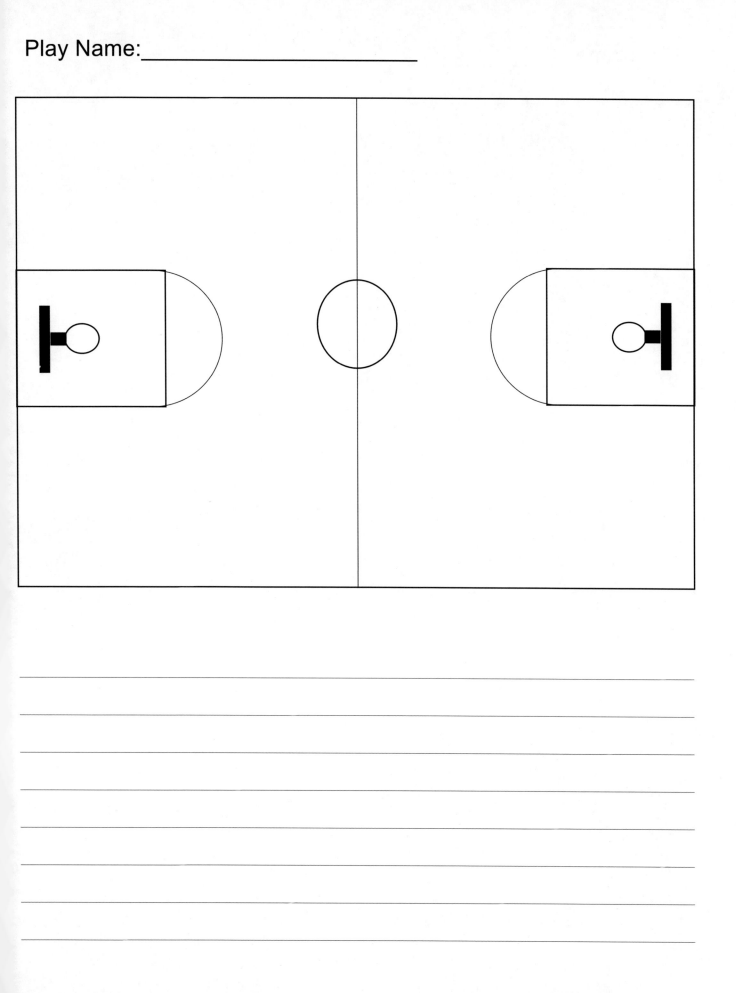

_____

_____

_____

_____

_____

_____

_____

_____

Play Name:_____

Play Name:_____

_____
_____
_____
_____
_____
_____
_____
_____

Play Name:_____

_____

_____

_____

_____

_____

_____

_____

_____

_____

_____

Play Name:_____

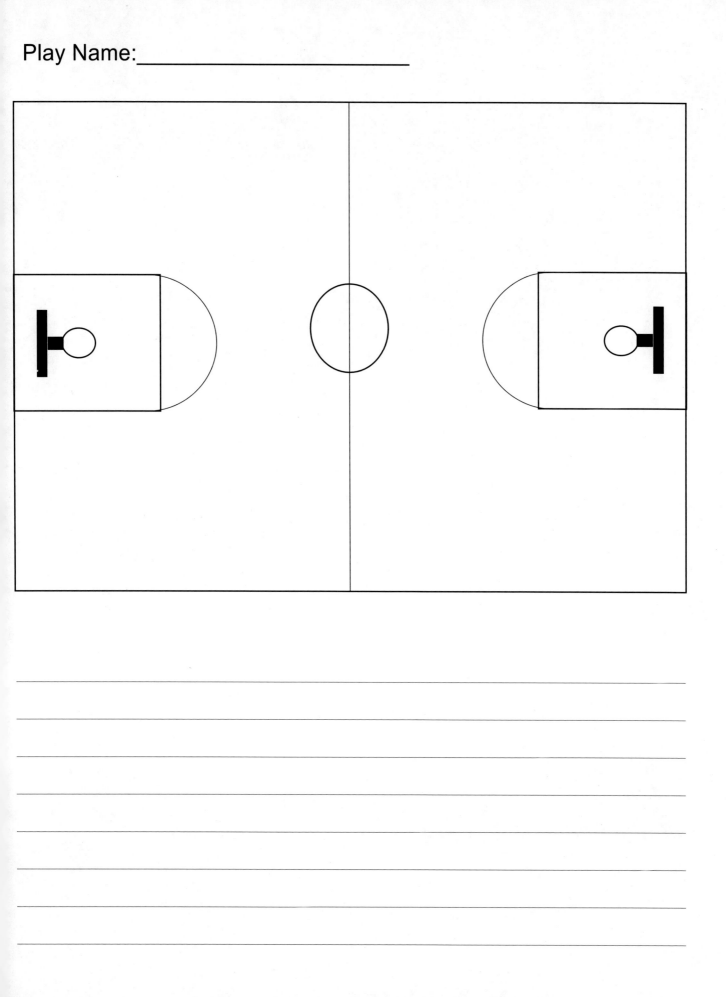

_____

_____

_____

_____

_____

_____

_____

Play Name:_____

Play Name:_____

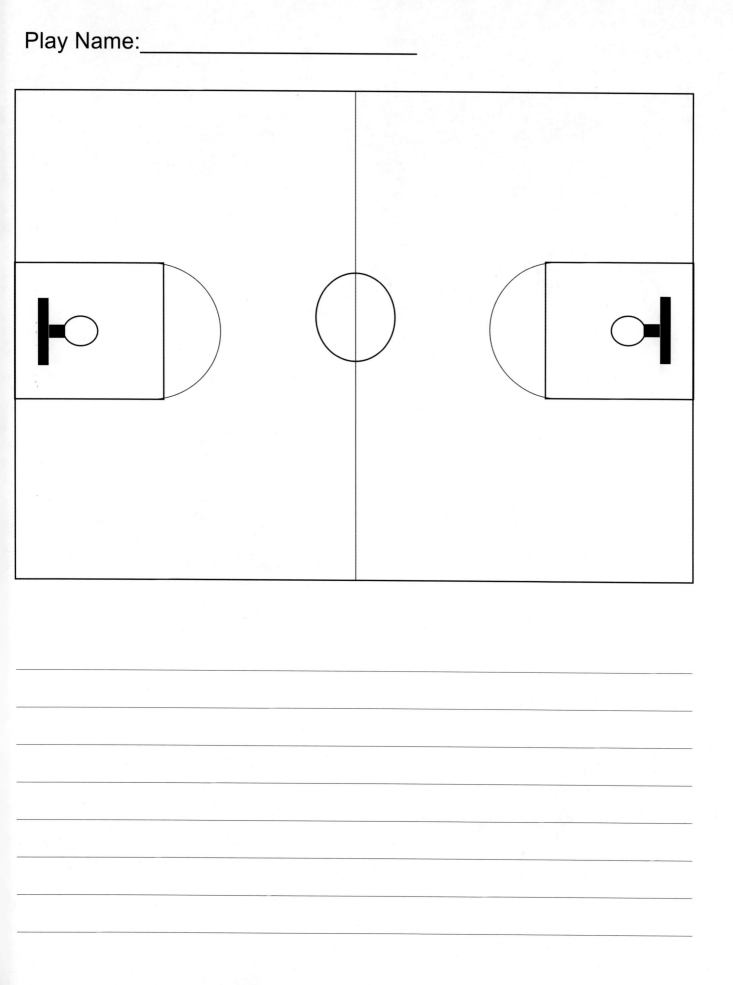

Play Name:_____

Statistics At A Glance

Date:_____   Opponent:_____   Home/Away

Player	#	Points	Rebounds	Assists	Steals	Blocks	Turnovers	Fouls	Total Points

Score

Halftime: Us_____ Them_____   Final: Us_____ Them_____

Statistics At A Glance

Date:_____   Opponent:_____   Home/Away

Player	#	Points	Rebounds	Assists	Steals	Blocks	Turnovers	Fouls	Total Points

Score

Halftime: Us_____ Them_____   Final: Us_____ Them_____

Statistics At A Glance

Date:_____   Opponent:_____   Home/Away

Player	#	Points	Rebounds	Assists	Steals	Blocks	Turnovers	Fouls	Total Points

Score

Halftime: Us_____ Them_____   Final: Us_____ Them_____

Statistics At A Glance

Date:_____   Opponent:_____   Home/Away

Player	#	Points	Rebounds	Assists	Steals	Blocks	Turnovers	Fouls	Total Points

Score

Halftime: Us_____ Them_____   Final: Us_____ Them_____

Statistics At A Glance

Date:_____   Opponent:_____   Home/Away

Player	#	Points	Rebounds	Assists	Steals	Blocks	Turnovers	Fouls	Total Points

Score

Halftime: Us_____ Them_____   Final: Us_____ Them_____

Statistics At A Glance

Date:_____   Opponent:_____   Home/Away

Player	#	Points	Rebounds	Assists	Steals	Blocks	Turnovers	Fouls	Total Points

Score

Halftime: Us_____ Them_____   Final: Us_____ Them_____

Statistics At A Glance

Date:_____   Opponent:_____   Home/Away

Player	#	Points	Rebounds	Assists	Steals	Blocks	Turnovers	Fouls	Total Points

Score

Halftime: Us_____ Them_____   Final: Us_____ Them_____

Statistics At A Glance

Date:_____   Opponent:_____   Home/Away

Player	#	Points	Rebounds	Assists	Steals	Blocks	Turnovers	Fouls	Total Points

Score

Halftime: Us_____ Them_____   Final: Us_____ Them_____

Statistics At A Glance

Date:_____ Opponent:_____ Home/Away

Player	#	Points	Rebounds	Assists	Steals	Blocks	Turnovers	Fouls	Total Points

Score

Halftime: Us_____ Them_____   Final: Us_____ Them_____

Statistics At A Glance

Date:_____   Opponent:_____   Home/Away

Player	#	Points	Rebounds	Assists	Steals	Blocks	Turnovers	Fouls	Total Points

Score

Halftime: Us_____ Them_____   Final: Us_____ Them_____

Statistics At A Glance

Date:_____   Opponent:_____   Home/Away

Player	#	Points	Rebounds	Assists	Steals	Blocks	Turnovers	Fouls	Total Points

Score

Halftime: Us_____ Them_____   Final: Us_____ Them_____

Statistics At A Glance

Date:_____   Opponent:_____   Home/Away

Player	#	Points	Rebounds	Assists	Steals	Blocks	Turnovers	Fouls	Total Points

Score

Halftime: Us_____ Them_____   Final: Us_____ Them_____

Statistics At A Glance

Date:_____   Opponent:_____   Home/Away

Player	#	Points	Rebounds	Assists	Steals	Blocks	Turnovers	Fouls	Total Points

Score

Halftime: Us_____ Them_____   Final: Us_____ Them_____

Statistics At A Glance

Date:_____   Opponent:_____   Home/Away

Player	#	Points	Rebounds	Assists	Steals	Blocks	Turnovers	Fouls	Total Points

Score

Halftime: Us_____ Them_____   Final: Us_____ Them_____

Statistics At A Glance

Date:_____   Opponent:_____   Home/Away

Player	#	Points	Rebounds	Assists	Steals	Blocks	Turnovers	Fouls	Total Points

Score

Halftime: Us_____ Them_____   Final: Us_____ Them_____

Statistics At A Glance

Date:_____   Opponent:_____   Home/Away

Player	#	Points	Rebounds	Assists	Steals	Blocks	Turnovers	Fouls	Total Points

Score

Halftime: Us_____ Them_____   Final: Us_____ Them_____

Statistics At A Glance

Date:_____   Opponent:_____   Home/Away

Player	#	Points	Rebounds	Assists	Steals	Blocks	Turnovers	Fouls	Total Points

Score

Halftime: Us_____ Them_____   Final: Us_____ Them_____

Statistics At A Glance

Date:_____   Opponent:_____   Home/Away

Player	#	Points	Rebounds	Assists	Steals	Blocks	Turnovers	Fouls	Total Points

Score

Halftime: Us_____ Them_____   Final: Us_____ Them_____

Statistics At A Glance

Date:_____   Opponent:_____   Home/Away

Player	#	Points	Rebounds	Assists	Steals	Blocks	Turnovers	Fouls	Total Points

Score

Halftime: Us_____ Them_____   Final: Us_____ Them_____

Statistics At A Glance

Date:_____   Opponent:_____   Home/Away

Player	#	Points	Rebounds	Assists	Steals	Blocks	Turnovers	Fouls	Total Points

Score

Halftime: Us_____ Them_____   Final: Us_____ Them_____

Statistics At A Glance

Date:_____   Opponent:_____   Home/Away

Player	#	Points	Rebounds	Assists	Steals	Blocks	Turnovers	Fouls	Total Points

Score

Halftime: Us_____ Them_____   Final: Us_____ Them_____

Statistics At A Glance

Date:_____   Opponent:_____   Home/Away

Player	#	Points	Rebounds	Assists	Steals	Blocks	Turnovers	Fouls	Total Points

Score
Halftime: Us_____ Them_____   Final: Us_____ Them_____

Statistics At A Glance

Date:_____   Opponent:_____   Home/Away

Player	#	Points	Rebounds	Assists	Steals	Blocks	Turnovers	Fouls	Total Points

Score

Halftime: Us_____ Them_____   Final: Us_____ Them_____

Statistics At A Glance

Date:_____   Opponent:_____   Home/Away

Player	#	Points	Rebounds	Assists	Steals	Blocks	Turnovers	Fouls	Total Points

Score

Halftime: Us_____ Them_____   Final: Us_____ Them_____

Statistics At A Glance

Date:_____   Opponent:_____   Home/Away

Player	#	Points	Rebounds	Assists	Steals	Blocks	Turnovers	Fouls	Total Points

Score

Halftime: Us_____ Them_____   Final: Us_____ Them_____

Statistics At A Glance

Date:_____   Opponent:_____   Home/Away

Player	#	Points	Rebounds	Assists	Steals	Blocks	Turnovers	Fouls	Total Points

Score

Halftime: Us_____ Them_____   Final: Us_____ Them_____

Statistics At A Glance

Date:_____   Opponent:_____   Home/Away

Player	#	Points	Rebounds	Assists	Steals	Blocks	Turnovers	Fouls	Total Points

Score

Halftime: Us_____ Them_____   Final: Us_____ Them_____

Statistics At A Glance

Date:_____   Opponent:_____   Home/Away

Player	#	Points	Rebounds	Assists	Steals	Blocks	Turnovers	Fouls	Total Points

Score

Halftime: Us_____ Them_____   Final: Us_____ Them_____

Statistics At A Glance

Date:_____   Opponent:_____   Home/Away

Player	#	Points	Rebounds	Assists	Steals	Blocks	Turnovers	Fouls	Total Points

Score

Halftime: Us_____ Them_____   Final: Us_____ Them_____

Statistics At A Glance

Date:_____   Opponent:_____   Home/Away

Player	#	Points	Rebounds	Assists	Steals	Blocks	Turnovers	Fouls	Total Points

Score
Halftime: Us_____ Them_____   Final: Us_____ Them_____

Statistics At A Glance

Date:_____   Opponent:_____   Home/Away

Player	#	Points	Rebounds	Assists	Steals	Blocks	Turnovers	Fouls	Total Points

Score

Halftime: Us_____ Them_____   Final: Us_____ Them_____

Statistics At A Glance

Date:_____   Opponent:_____   Home/Away

Player	#	Points	Rebounds	Assists	Steals	Blocks	Turnovers	Fouls	Total Points

Score

Halftime: Us_____ Them_____   Final: Us_____ Them_____

Statistics At A Glance

Date:_____   Opponent:_____   Home/Away

Player	#	Points	Rebounds	Assists	Steals	Blocks	Turnovers	Fouls	Total Points

Score

Halftime: Us_____ Them_____   Final: Us_____ Them_____

Statistics At A Glance

Date:_____   Opponent:_____   Home/Away

Player	#	Points	Rebounds	Assists	Steals	Blocks	Turnovers	Fouls	Total Points

Score

Halftime: Us_____ Them_____   Final: Us_____ Them_____

Statistics At A Glance

Date:_____   Opponent:_____   Home/Away

Player	#	Points	Rebounds	Assists	Steals	Blocks	Turnovers	Fouls	Total Points

Score

Halftime: Us_____ Them_____   Final: Us_____ Them_____

Statistics At A Glance

Date:_____   Opponent:_____   Home/Away

Player	#	Points	Rebounds	Assists	Steals	Blocks	Turnovers	Fouls	Total Points

Score

Halftime: Us_____ Them_____   Final: Us_____ Them_____

Statistics At A Glance

Date:_____   Opponent:_____   Home/Away

Player	#	Points	Rebounds	Assists	Steals	Blocks	Turnovers	Fouls	Total Points

Score

Halftime: Us_____ Them_____   Final: Us_____ Them_____

Statistics At A Glance

Date:_____   Opponent:_____   Home/Away

Player	#	Points	Rebounds	Assists	Steals	Blocks	Turnovers	Fouls	Total Points

Score

Halftime: Us_____ Them_____   Final: Us_____ Them_____

Statistics At A Glance

Date:_____   Opponent:_____   Home/Away

Player	#	Points	Rebounds	Assists	Steals	Blocks	Turnovers	Fouls	Total Points

Score

Halftime: Us_____ Them_____   Final: Us_____ Them_____

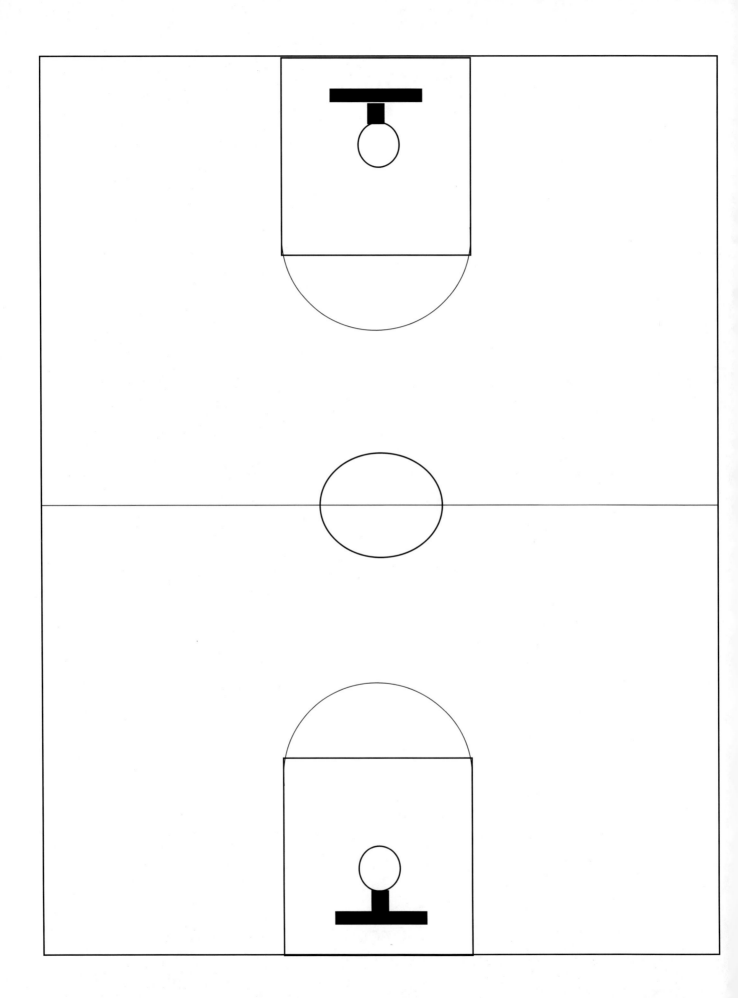

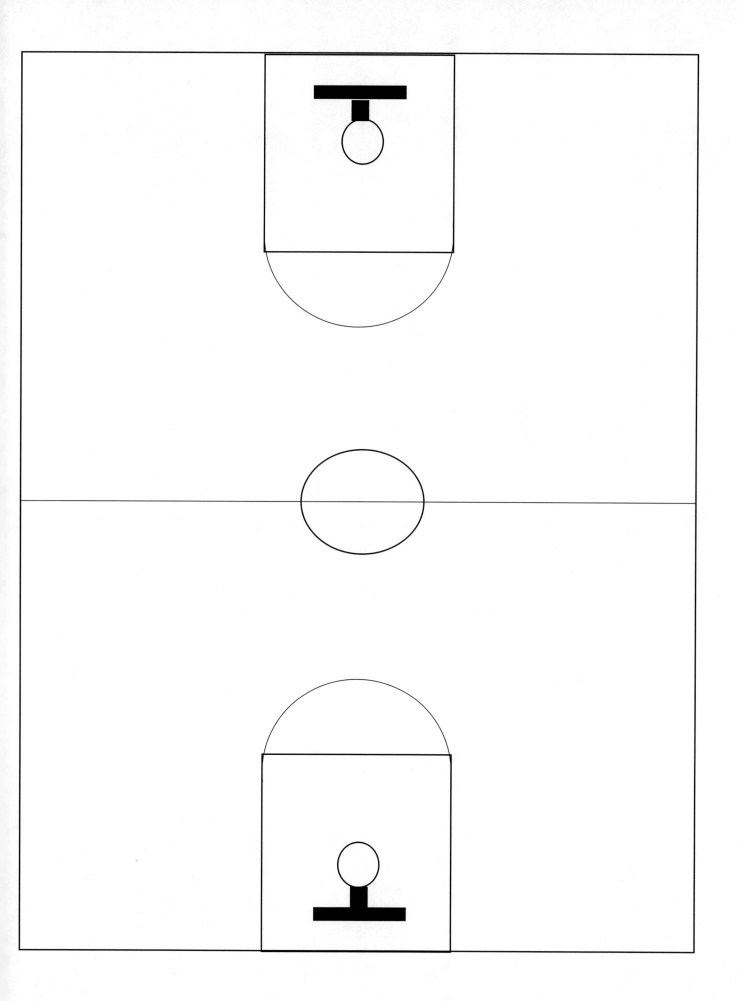

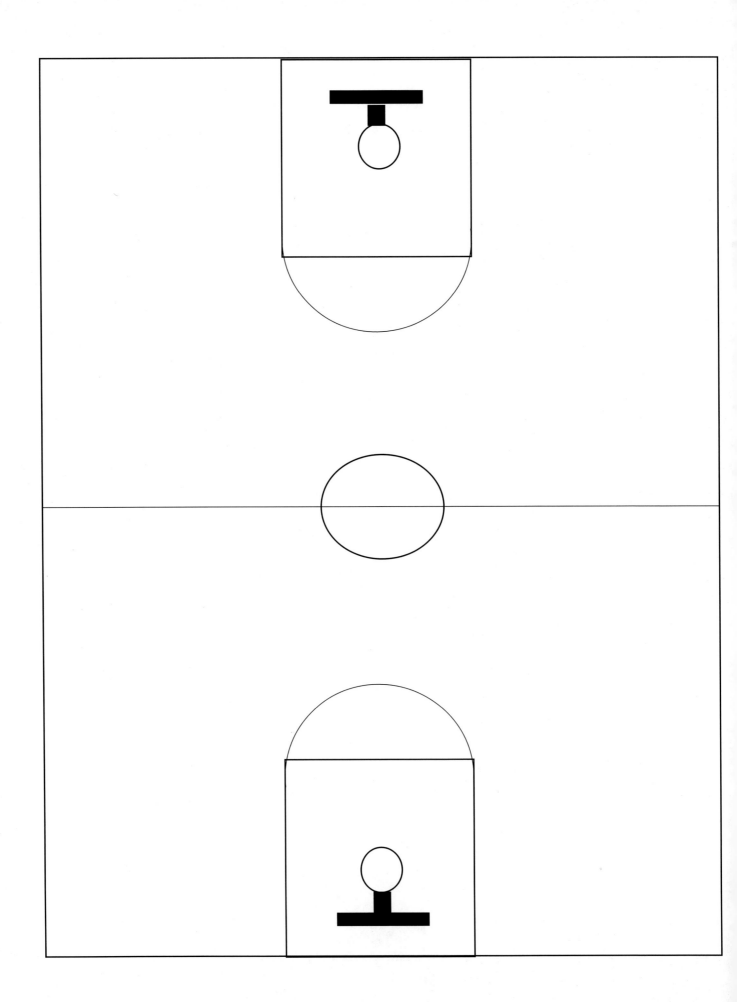

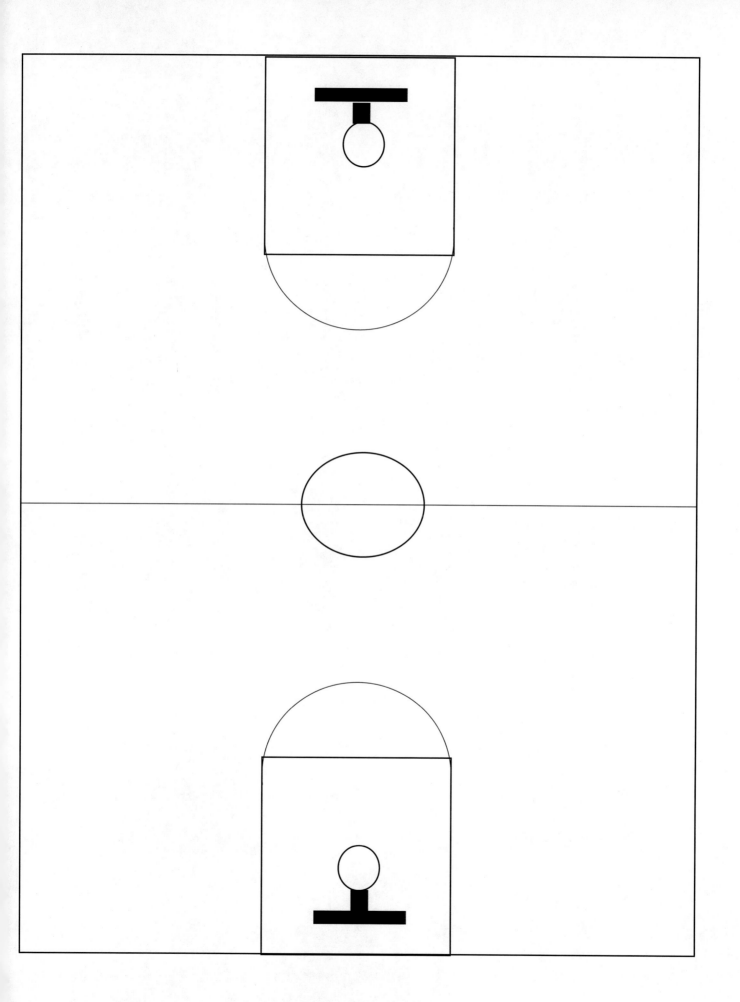

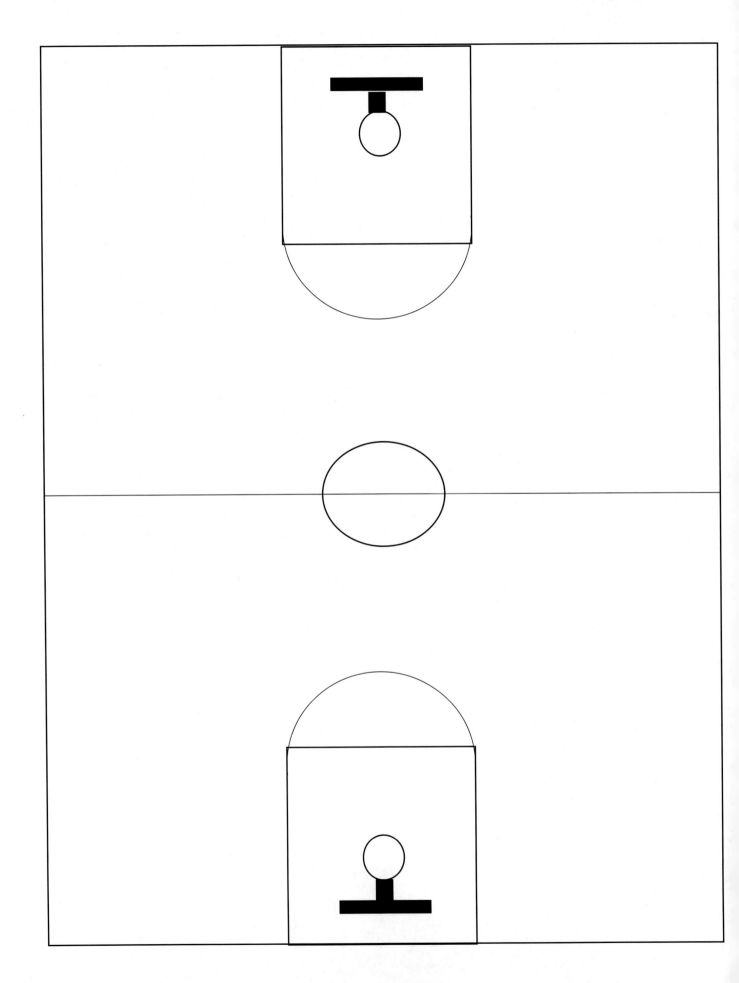

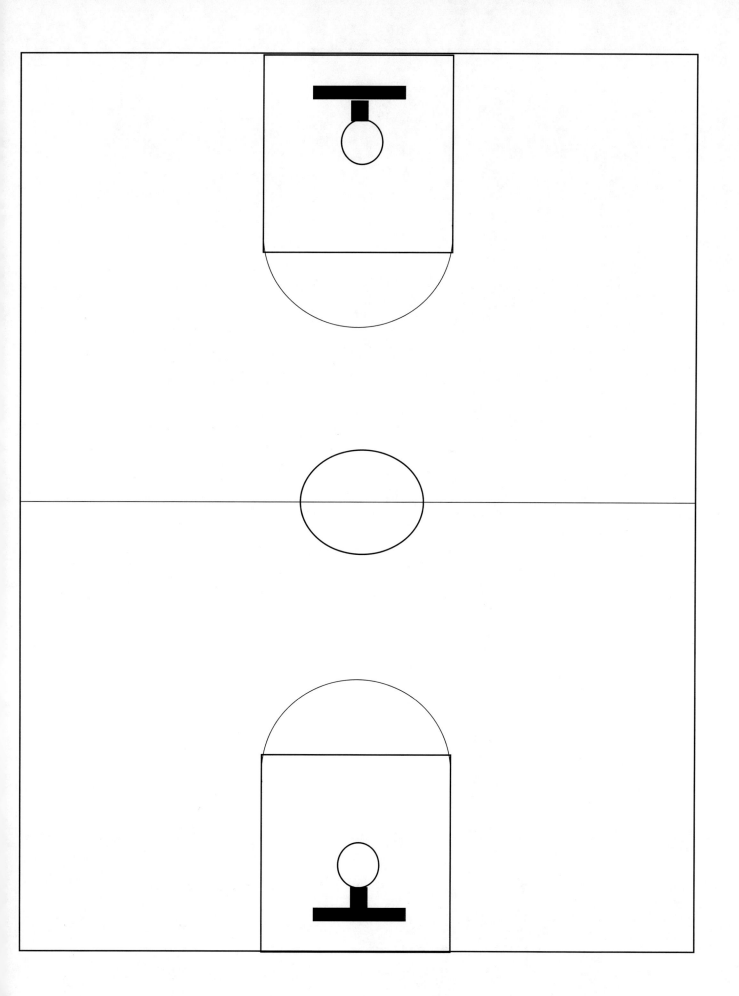

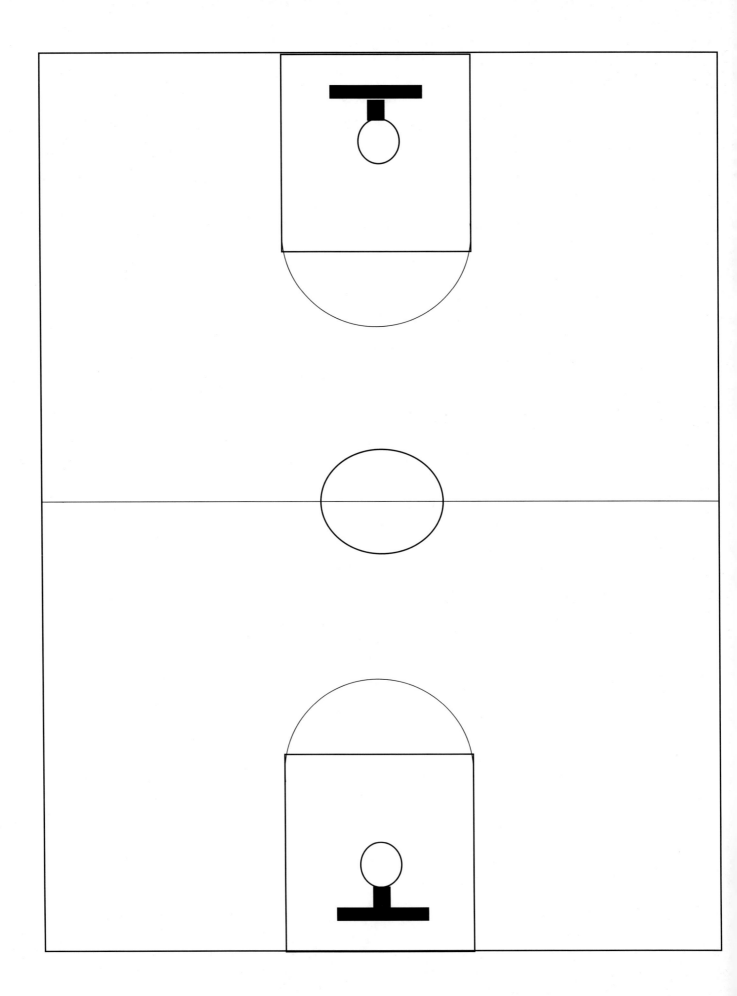

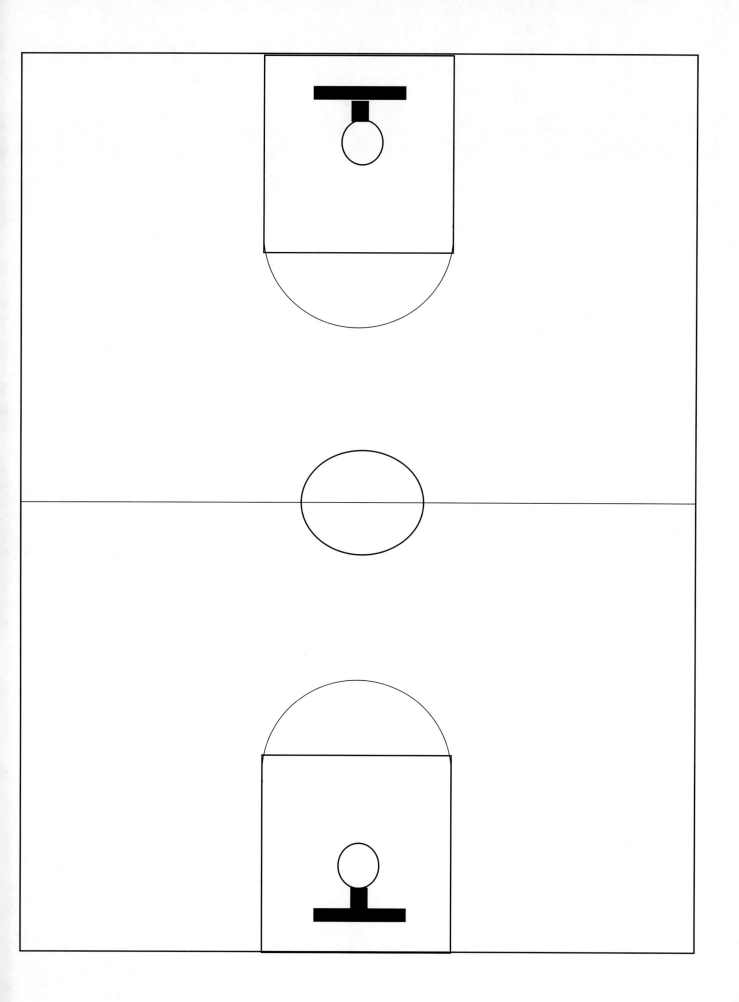

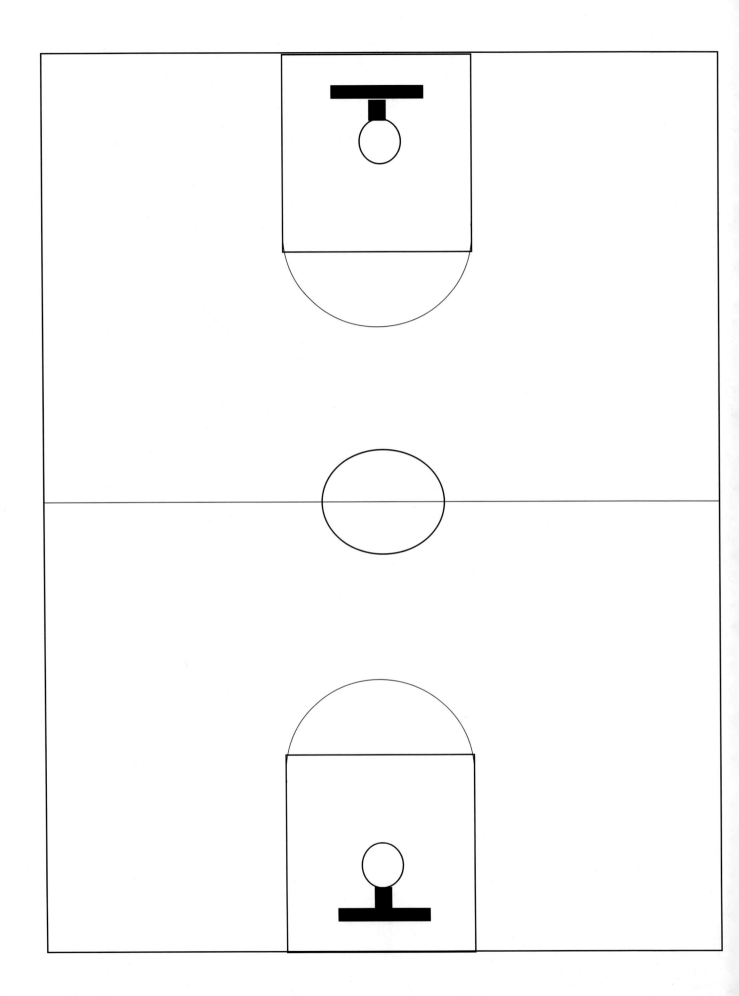

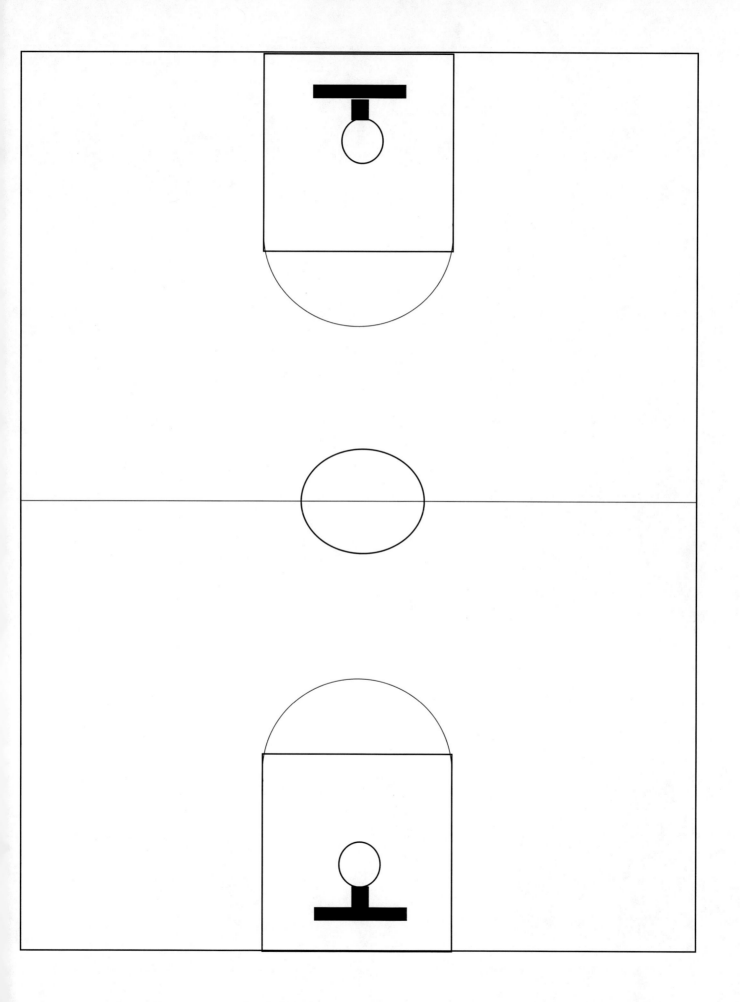

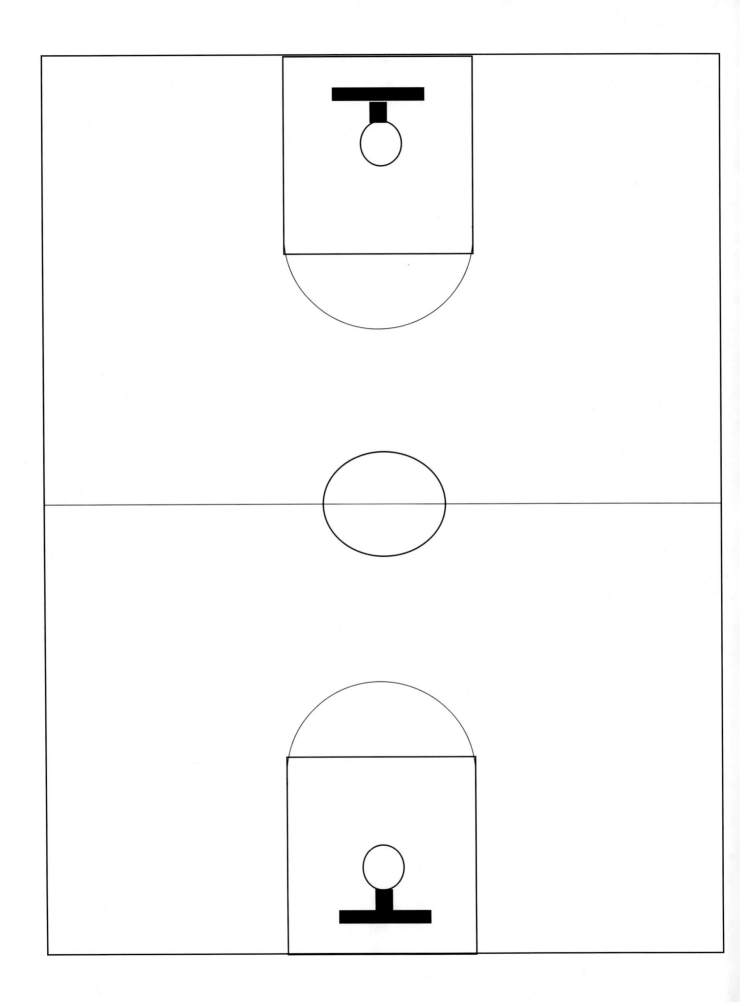

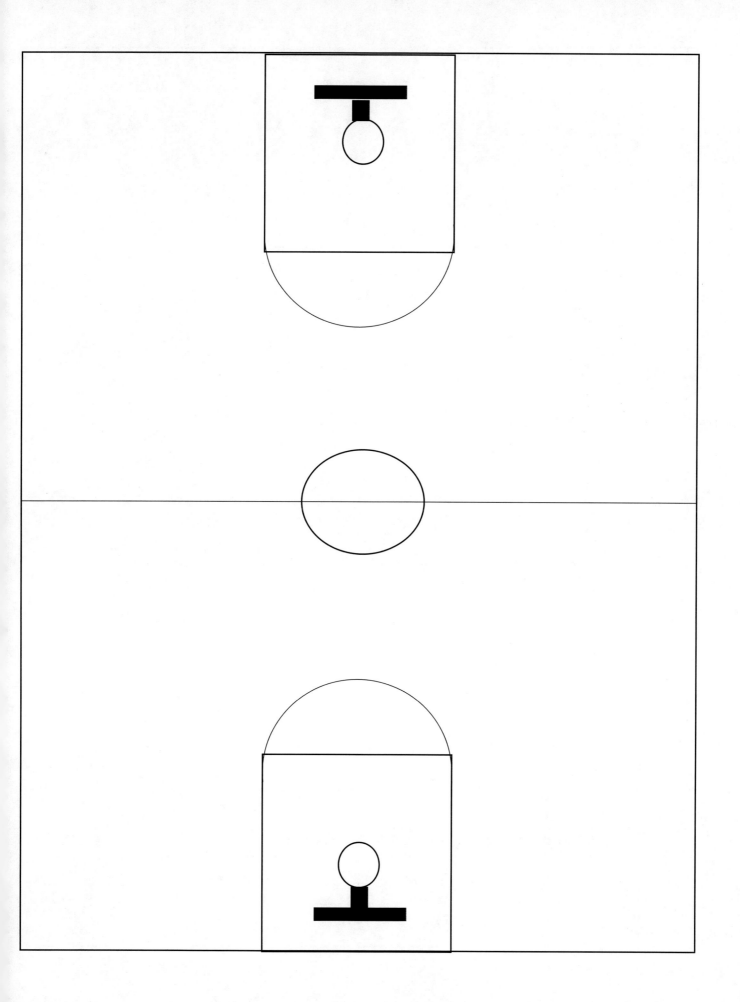

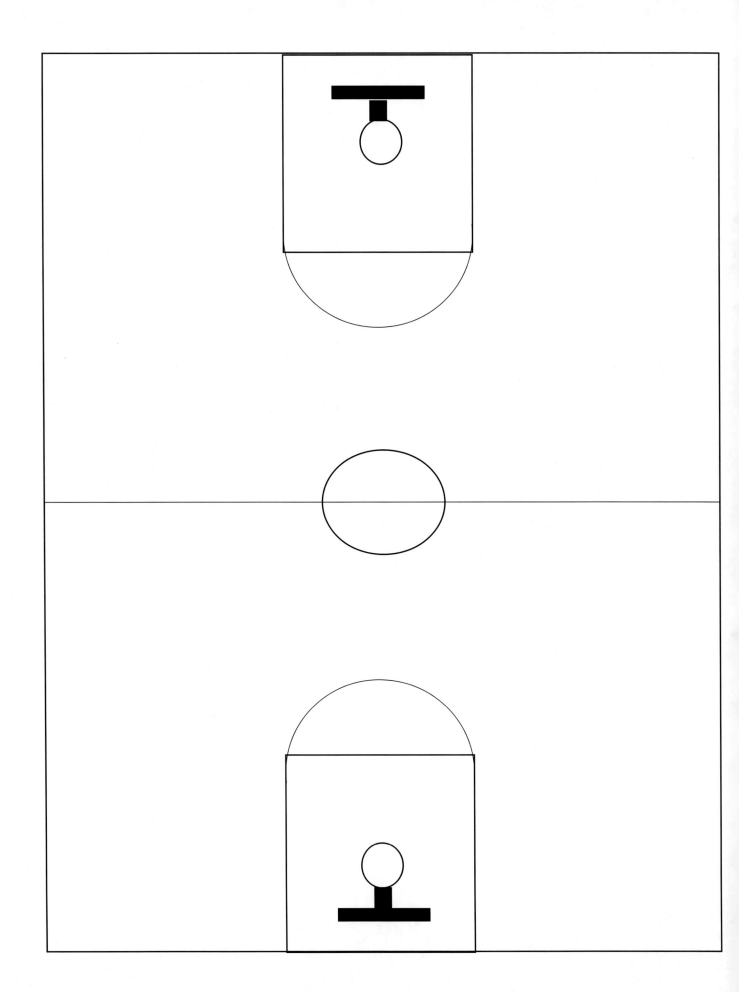

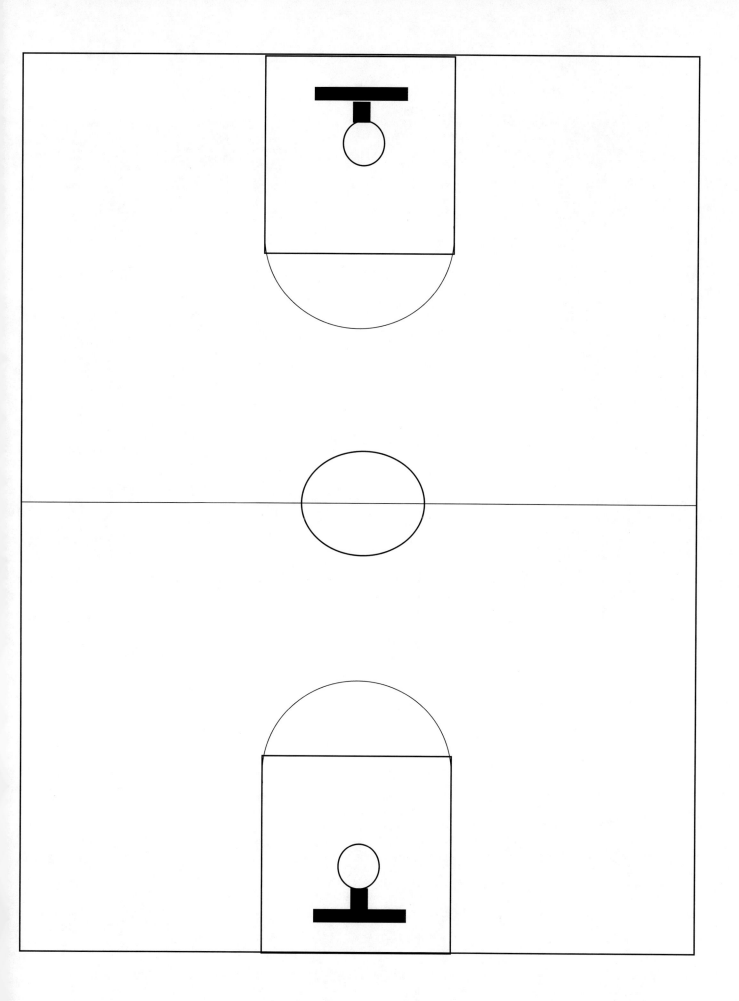

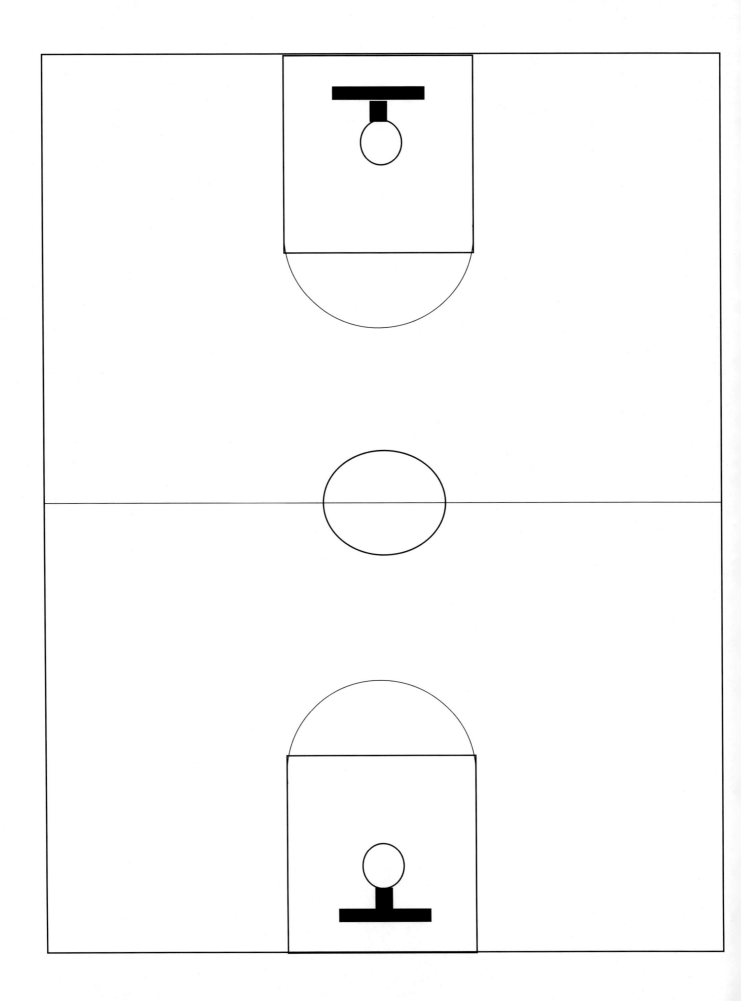

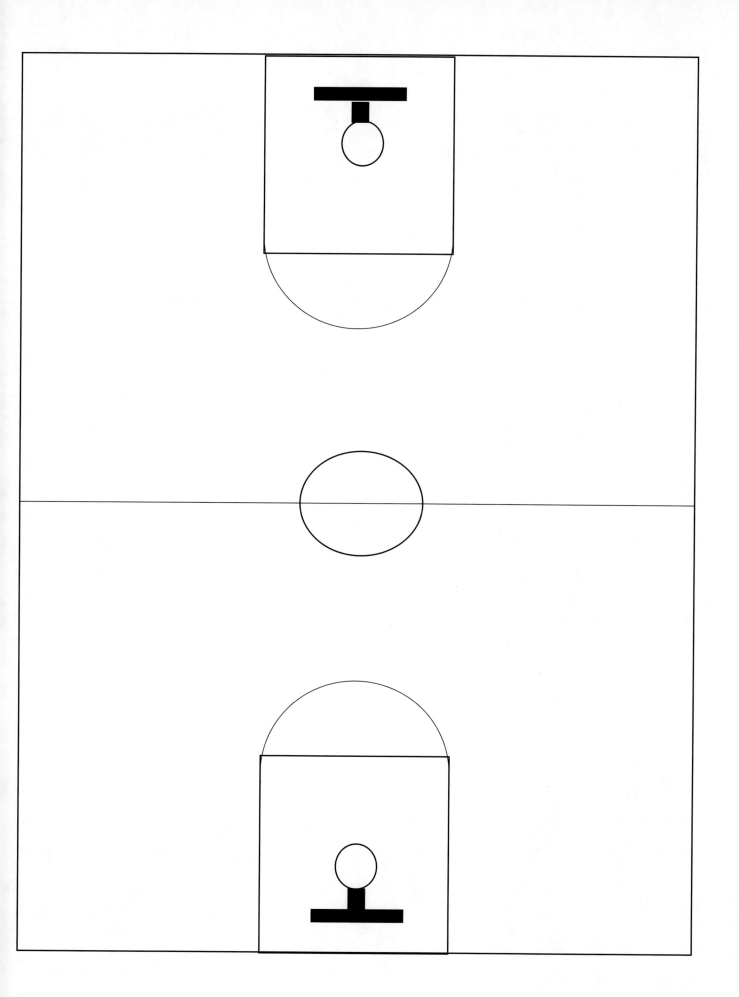

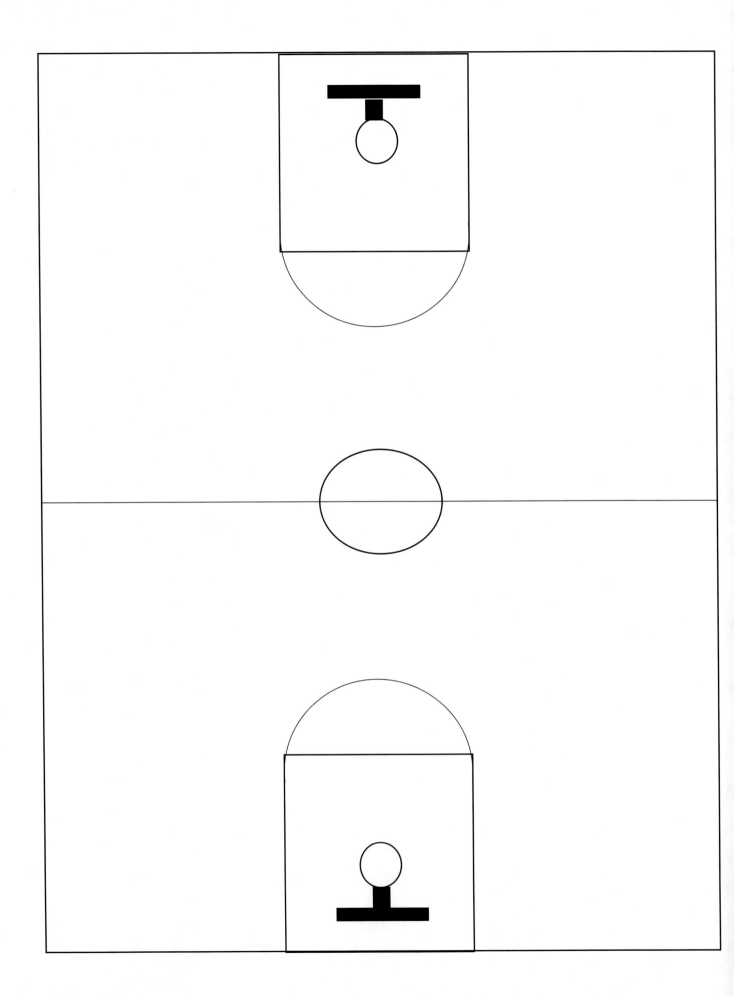

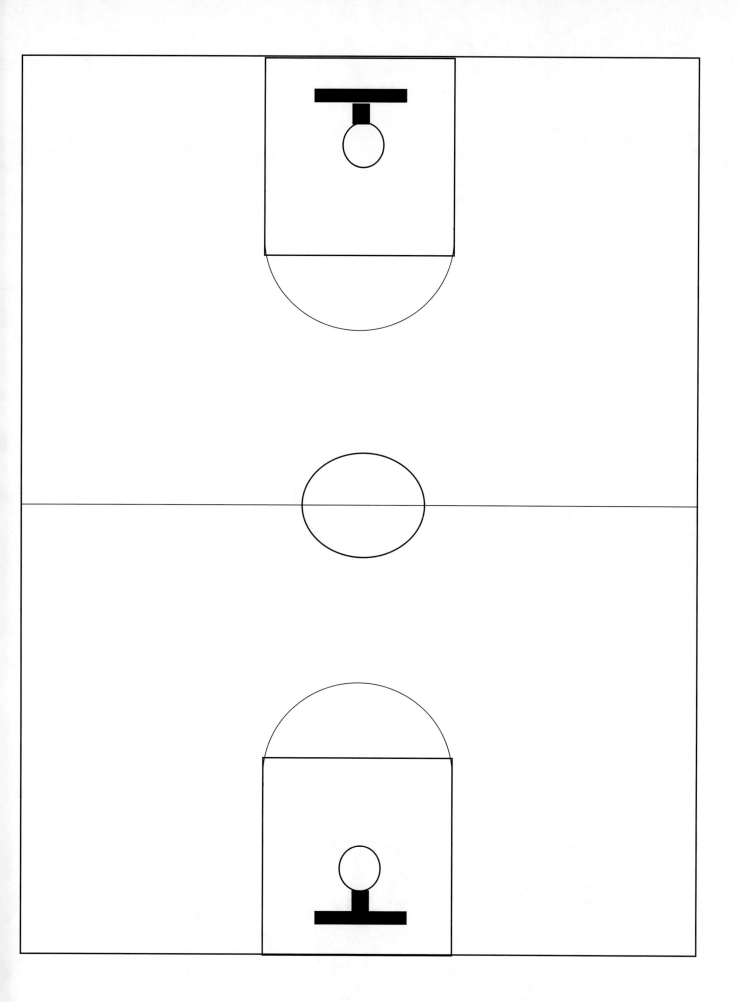

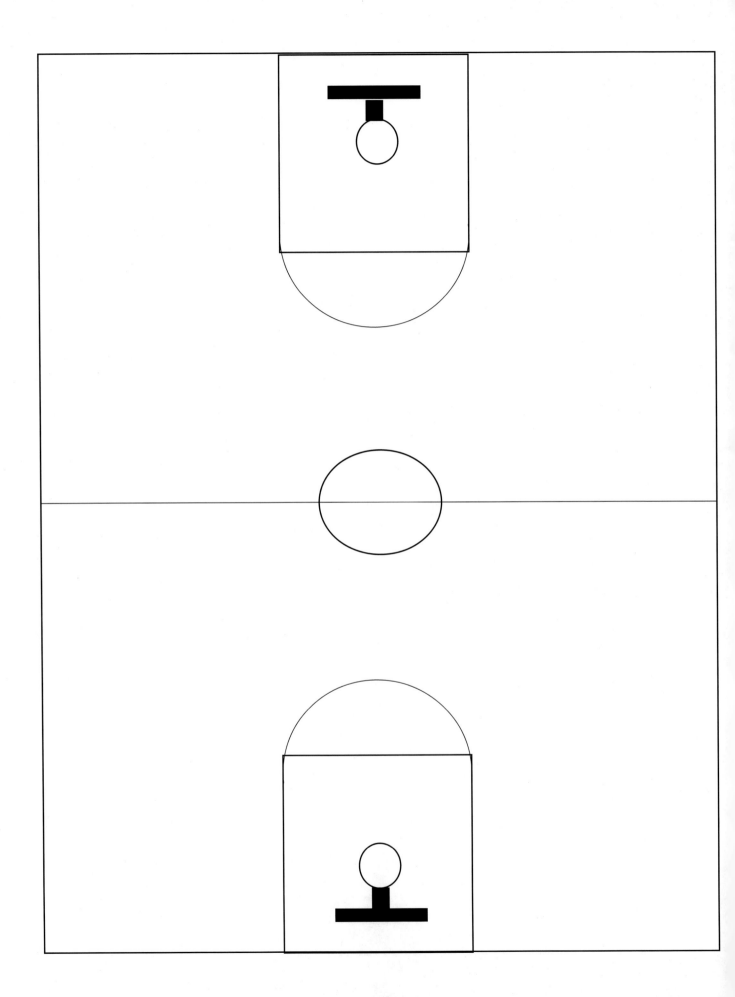

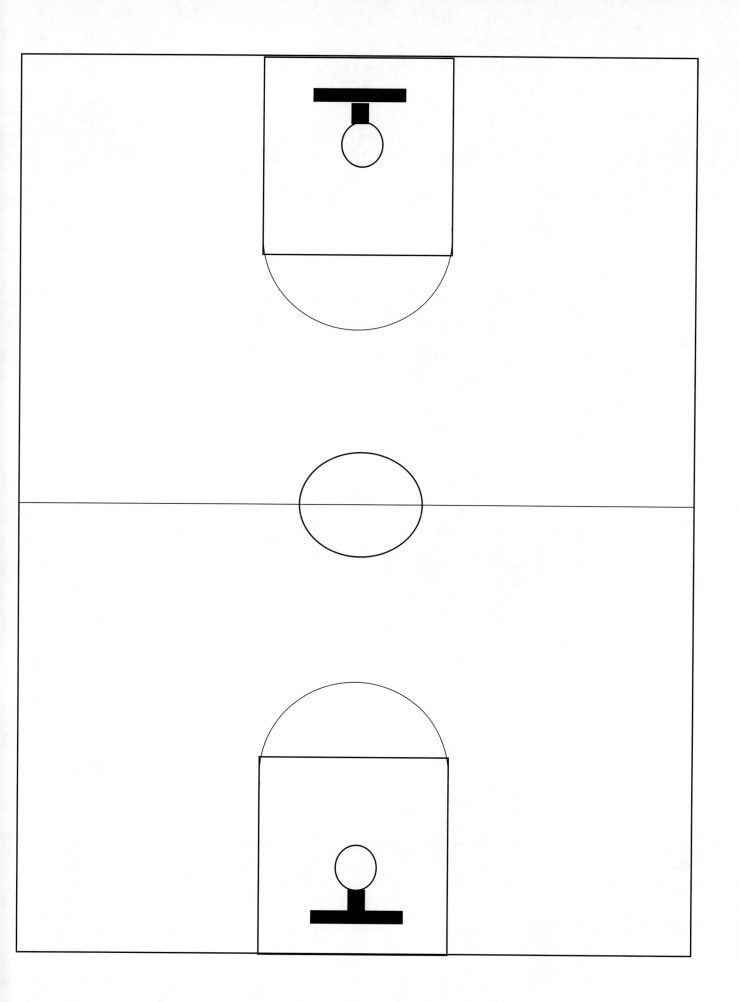

Notes

Notes

Notes

Notes

Notes

Notes

Notes

Notes

Notes

Notes

Notes

Manufactured by Amazon.ca
Acheson, AB

15899497R00061